THE HIDDEN HIMALAYAS

PHOTOGRAPHS BY THOMAS L. KELLY

TEXT BY V. CARROLL DUNHAM

ABBEVILLE PRESS PUBLISHERS NEW YORK

Editor: Alan Axelrod
Designer: Nai Chang
Production Supervisor: Hope Koturo

Frontispieces:

Humla Bhotia greeting and farewell gesture.
With a deference acknowledging the divine
Buddha nature, the master, with open hands,
receives his younger lama disciple.

Simikot village, fall, winter, spring, and summer.

Lobsong Lama erects a *lungta*, a Buddhist
prayer flag, in the highland summer pastures.
Lungta, which means "windhorse," is said to
broadcast the word of the Dharma (Buddhist
law) to all who pass near.

DEDICATION PAGE

Lobsong Lama, the Nyingmapa monk of Yakba.

A C K N O W L E D G M E N T S

I am greatly indebted to many people for their help and generosity in the preparation
of this book. It all started with Tom Cox's invitation to join him in Humla. His ability
with the Tibetan language, his humor, and his inquisitive nature were invaluable.

Without the friendship of Boom Lama, Tashi Doma, Eppi, Tshewang Lama and
his family, I might not have had the inspiration and energy to continue.

Many thanks to Jane Osborne-Fellows, Iain Oswald, Almerie Colloredo, my parents—
Bud and Jeanne Kelly—and my brother, Bob, for their kindness and support during
my difficult initiation into publishing.

I owe special thanks to Lisa Rush. She has molded this project in many ways.

V. Carroll Dunham deserves the most thanks. Her companionship, compassionate
nature, and sensitive skill as a writer helped make this dream come true.

THOMAS L. KELLY

Library of Congress Cataloging-in-Publication Data

Kelly, Thomas L.
    The hidden Himalayas.

    1. Jumla (Nepal: District)—Description and travel
—Views. I. Dunham, V. Carroll. II. Title.
DS495.8.J85K45 1987   954.9'6   87-948
ISBN 0-89659-758-X

Printed in Japan

To Lobsong Lama "The Blessed One" 1912–1986

PREFACE

In February 1984 I came to Nepal bearing a camera for a friend of a friend. The camera was for Tom Kelly, a former Peace Corps worker and CARE development program officer from Santa Fe, New Mexico, who, at the time, was struggling to establish himself as a free-lance photographer and audio-visual technician.

I remember our first dinner together. He could hardly contain himself as he described his recent adventure in the remote northwest district of Humla. The fire in Tom Kelly's eyes was telling—for a six-year veteran of Nepal's mountains. Fluent in Nepali, Tom had spent two years in eastern Nepal building drinking-water systems and a year-and-a-half scouting potential bridge-building sites throughout the country. I knew this place called Humla must be special.

Learning that I shared his interest in documenting the rich traditions of remote regions, Tom asked me to join him when he returned to Humla. But that would have to wait. A cultural anthropology major at Princeton, I had come to Nepal for field research on the psychoanalytic aspects of the Vajrayana monastic tradition. After a six-month sojourn in a Buddhist nunnery learning the Tibetan language, I returned to Princeton to complete my degree.

When I returned to Nepal in the fall of 1985, Tom again asked me to accompany him to Humla. "There's lots of nuns up there," he said.

I joined him, and together we shared a lifetime of experiences. This book is a tribute to those people in this haunting region who touched our hearts and souls as we shared with them the cycle of the seasons.

CONTENTS

INTRODUCTION

Humla. The word resonates like a hymn. Vast and humbling, Humla echoes in whispers. Humla is powerful, yet elusive, like the roar of the Karnali River carving and curling its way through the massifs that isolate and protect this lonely Himalayan region. Nestled between the sweltering Indian subcontinent and the frozen plains of the Tibetan plateau, Humla lies hidden in the far northwest corner of Nepal. Shadows of the towering Saipal range and sacred Takh and Changla Himals loom over this barren, forgotten land. The sweeping wind of Humla evokes wistful thoughts for a way of life destined eventually to perish.

Through the ageless mountain corridors, the Hindu Chhetris, Thakuris, and Buddhist Bhotias of Humla continue to listen to the vanishing rhythms of an ancient heritage, despite their dwindling means of survival. Cultivatable land grows scarcer as the population increases, the ancient salt and wool trade has lost much of its economic significance, and encroaching modern culture threatens to replace traditional beliefs. In the Diamond Sutra Buddha says, "Thus shall you think of all this fleeting world: A star at dawn, a bubble in a stream, a flash of lightning in a summer cloud, a flickering lamp, a phantom and a dream." If the people here were to pick up and move on, scars on the rough landscape would be few. Yet a faint reverberation would linger, refusing to be forgotten. An ancient way of being permeates the rarified air.

We have taken strands of our fleeting impressions and woven them together by season. We ventured to this harsh land to listen to the vanishing rhythms of human striving, struggle, and celebration. Each season in Humla presents an entirely separate world of sensations, activities, harmonies, and colors. Summer was to winter as the flash of lightning to the flickering lamp. Here the cycle of the seasons dictates the pattern of celebration and struggle. The act of survival becomes a concentrated meditation in reverent harmony with the natural elements.

Humla's Tapestry

Remote, impoverished, Humla is forgotten by all but those who live there. Criss-crossed with pilgrimage paths and ancient trade routes, Humla has rarely been a destination itself. Few have bothered to discover the pattern of existence in this faded tapestry of landscape and cultures: the weft of valleys, the warp of mountains, the weft of Hindu Chhetris and Thakuris, the warp of Buddhist Bhotias.

Like the hazy smoke that hovers over village rooftops at dawn, Humla's history disappears into an obscure mist of legend and lore. During the early Moghul invasions of the thirteenth century, Hindu Chhetri and Thakuri ancestors of warrior and royal caste fled the desert lowlands of Rajasthan, finding refuge in Humla's valleys. Along with traditional customs and garb, like the bulbous white turban and elegant mustache, white gowns for unmarried virgins, and cowrie shells from the Bay of Bengal for women to weave into their long black hair, they brought with them ancient Rajasthani

Torpu Eppi spinning wool.

11

gods, language, and folk beliefs—gone now from Rajasthan itself.

The Chhetris and Thakuris found Humla settled by the native Khas people, an Indo-Aryan tribe believed to have first traveled through Humla trading pecans and cloth from their native Persia and Kashmir. The Khasa kings formed the famous Malla Kingdom, which ruled Humla from the eleventh century before collapsing and splintering into local chiefdoms during the fourteenth century. Practicing an animist religion called Masta, the Khas soon began to intermarry with the immigrant Chhetris and Thakuris.

With superior political and military organization and their traditional ruling status, the Thakuris quickly dominated the area, forming the Kalyal confederacy, which ruled Humla until the Gurkha conquest and unification of Nepal in 1768. Secluded from Brahmanic centers of thought, a unique folk Hinduism emerged in Humla, fusing elements of Masta animism with orthodox Hindu beliefs.

The Hindu's religious landscape is alive with gods and spirits of the land, water, and sky. Both benevolent and malevolent, these gods control fate and destiny, harvests and fertility. Manifesting themselves through a human oracle, a village shaman called the *dhami*, the spirits speak and live. Shaking violently while possessed, the dhami is the incarnation of the particular divinity he represents. A *pujari*, acting as interpreter, explains the significance of the deity's words as spoken by the dhami. Villagers consult the dhami on matters of illness, poor crops, marriage, love, business, and misfortune.

But the gods do not speak to the Hindus alone. Throughout the last eight centuries, in overlapping migrations from the north, the Bhotias—Tibetan-speaking people of Tibetan origin—have trickled south from the Asiatic steppes, settling Humla's highlands above ten thousand feet. While the Hindus, originally from the Indian plains, prefer valleys and riverbeds, the mountains are home to the Buddhists.

Bon, a religion with archaic roots in Siberian-Mongolian shamanism and influences derived from Persian Zoroastrianism and Indian Saivism, flourished in Humla before the advent of Buddhism in the fourteenth century. Humla's Bhotia world is alive with stories of wandering Buddhist saints who conquered the many pre-Buddhist Bon deities and demons of the region.

Both popular saints, Padmasambhava and Milarepa, are immortalized in legend and shrines for their deeds in the area. Their lasting influence is felt by the large numbers of devout Buddhist lamas, monks, and nuns of the ancient Nyingmapa sect, who weave subsistence and ritual together in lives of hard work and faith.

Practicing a folk Buddhism that incorporates local deities and ancestor worship, the villagers continue to trust old rites that give them control over supernatural beings and the powers around them. They do not entirely grasp the involved theology or sublimities of orthodox Buddhism. Steady waves of Tibetan Buddhist practice have washed over the Bon tradition, rendering it faint.

Shamanism and animal sacrifice persist in some Bhotia villages, where a dhami sacrifices animals to local as well as Buddhist deities. (Many dhamis attempt to disguise their practices with a thin veneer of orthodox Buddhism, sacrificing only symbolic animals molded from flour.)

The last sign of the fading Bon tradition is the distinctive topknot, reminiscent of the hairdo of Hindu ascetics and Bon shamans but unique to Humla and quickly becoming extinct. At one time all men in Humla wore their hair this way. It is believed they store secret magical weapons of power inside the raised knot, which is called a *tarchok*, the same word as for a prayer flagpole, since, jutting from the head, it catches the breeze in a similar fashion.

Nowhere in the Himalayas have Hindus and Buddhists coexisted so intimately for so long with as little trace of religious syncretism. In the tapestry of Humla, the Hindu weft and the Buddhist warp are interwoven yet remain distinct.

Despite a shared environment, the Hindus and Buddhists live by almost diametrically opposed values and codes of behavior. The Thakuris and Chhetris follow the orthodox Hindu principle of judging actions according to a scale of purity and pollution, whereas the Bhotias are more relaxed, freely drinking fermented barley beer, eating meat, and allowing a great deal of sexual freedom.

Nevertheless, the Hindu world seems softer than that of the Bhotias. The women embody an enigmatic femininity. Shy, yet seductive and sensuous, they quietly move through the landscape, swinging their hips as they carry bundles of wood or brass pots on their heads. Silent except among themselves, they hide behind mysterious veils. Nose rings glisten, bangles and thick silver ankle bracelets jingle as they rustle across barren fields in long pleated skirts.

Hindus are wary of strangers; their world can be elusive, at times inaccessible, and they themselves can be sullen, brooding, suspicious, and superstitious. With thin regal bodies and chiseled Aryan features, liquid brown eyes, and hair glistening with mustard oil, these people who seem to whisper when they talk, evoke a haunting gentleness.

The Bhotias are hardier—brash, boisterous, forthright, and bold. With Mongolian eyes that belie origins in the Asiatic steppes, the Bhotias are more solid than the willow-framed Hindus. Wearing practical knickers and jumper tunics, chests adorned with enormous hunks of turquoise and amulets to ward off evil spirits, the Bhotia women exude an independence, strength, and quick wit not readily found among the more reticent Chhetris. The Bhotias are trustworthy, yet they are shrewd traders and more prosperous than the Hindus.

Social life among the Bhotias has a complexity all its own. The rare practice of fraternal polyandry (two or more brothers married to the same wife) curbs population growth, concentrates the wealth of each household by maintaining a larger population of working adult males under each roof, and prevents the dispersal of land and possessions. In an area of scarce resources, the monogamous Hindus are much poorer because of their larger families and smaller land plots. Indeed, one wonders how the ever-infertile fields support the land's inhabitants. This sea of forgotten mountains scarcely seems a place for human habitation. Both Hindus and Bhotias grow millet, buckwheat, potatoes, turnips, and barley, but the yield from the stubborn alpine soil is meager, forcing them to resort to seasonal herding and trading trips to make up for chronic harvest deficits. Vestiges of the ancient trans-Himalayan salt and wool trade persist, as caravans of yaks and goats loaded with grains, salt, and wool, traverse the beaten trails.

The rhythm of fall begins with the pounding of harvest grains. Stalks of copper buckwheat, yak blankets full of amaranth, millet, and barley dry on manure-mud rooftops, bathed in the amber light of autumn. Chaffing and winnowing grains, the mood is one of preparation for the long winter months ahead. At a traders' fair, Bhotias and Hindus meet with Limi Tibetans from the far northern region of Humla to barter for essential winter provisions. Traveling with the Limi traders, we join their yak caravan north to celebrate the harvest and participate in the grand festivities of a polyandrous wedding, abundant with silk brocade, muskrat fur, and barrels of barley beer.

Winter in Humla is refuge. The frozen silence of the alpine terrain blanketed in white penetrates the soul. People seem hushed and walk on tiptoe, seeking solace beside the hearth—with each other or alone in silent contemplation. One can almost hear the mountains tremble in the lonely cold. Despite the unbearable weather, the cycle of necessary tasks—gathering water, fetching wood, shoveling rooftops—must continue.

Washing away the grime and sobriety of winter, spring is a rebirth, a melting of snow accompanied by giggles, gossip, and the exuberant masked drama called *Mani*. Spring is flirtatious, boisterous, and outrageous. Spring is a time for sowing fields, the jubilant reunion of sheep caravans returning from trading trips south, and kids playing underneath a shower of plum-blossom petals.

Summer is easy, summer is lazy, summer is green and lush, a time to yawn and stretch out in the high pastures of alpine wildflowers, watching grazing yaks and sheep, or spinning wool, churning butter, and drying cheese. Shepherdesses daydream, and caravans of yaks carry lumber up to the Tibetan plateau. Dhamis gather during the full moon in August to worship and rejoice, affirming ties of brotherhood while appeasing and propitiating the gods. The air turns brisk, and the faint echo of pounding grain once again fills this lonely land.

Like the destiny of an echo lost in the mountains, the hymn of Humla's ancient ways is fated to perish. Or is it? Where does a season go when its time has passed? Like a bubble in a stream or a flash of lightning in a summer cloud, this world is constant flux. Winter dies and spring is reborn. The people of Humla will adopt new rhythms of existence. Will the poetry of their hard life be lost, or will it merely be absorbed by the canyon walls and snow peaks? If we just learn to listen, we will hear the whisper of a way of life hidden in the Himalayas.

FALL

Fall descends upon Humla.
The thump of wooden pestles pounding grain
echoes through the mountains.
Golden bosch-tree leaves dance in the wind,
and the mountain shadows stretch longer
over the basin valleys.

18

Smoke from morning fires hovers above the Chhetri village of Simikot. In a land of no electricity and little fuel, villagers retire early and rise with the sun. *Simikot* means "court above the bean marsh," for it was here, four hundred years ago, that a Thakuri prince ruled the Kalyal confederacy. Today, Simikot is the district center of Humla, housing many government offices, two schools, a medical outpost, and a police headquarters that guards the Nepalese–Chinese border. Simikot also possesses the region's only link with Nepal's capital city of Kathmandu—an airstrip.

Dwarfed by the towering Lekh Dharma mountains, Chhetri children dance in the rising mist before gathering potatoes. A prized crop, the potato has a relatively brief history in the Himalayas. During the late 1800s the wife of a British administrator in Darjeeling, India, planted potatoes in her garden. Her Sherpa servant brought some back to his village, thus adding the plant to the list of Himalayan staples.

Bhotia children toss drying turnips to the wind in an exuberant morning ballet. In a land of vertical mountains, flat rooftops serve the dual function of playground and workspace. Rooftops are ideal for drying turnips, a staple in winter stews.

Morning contemplation. In a religious culture, time for reflection is as important as work. Nomdyol, the fourteen-year-old granddaughter of Lobsong Lama, looks below to the village of Yakba from her monastery home. A Buddhist prayer flag flutters in the wind nearby.

Surrounded by earthen pots of fermenting barley beer *(chang),* an old Bhotia man of the village of Brassi wears the traditional topknot hairdo, called the *tarchok*—the same word as for prayer-flagpole; it juts from the head in a similar fashion. Nowadays, the hairdo is held together by a sharp, protruding needle, though it is believed that Humla's nomadic Bonpo shaman ancestors once stuck tent pegs in the hair as magical weapons. Humla is the last area in which tarchoks persist. A symbol of spiritual power and strength, the tarchok is believed to protect the wearer from evil spirits. Outside of Humla, orthodox Tibetan Buddhists no longer wear tarchoks to hide magical weapons. Instead, the shaman's tent peg has evolved into the *phurba* or "magic dart" and no longer serves as a weapon against external demons, but as a symbol by which the "demon of the ego, or deluded self" is slain.

A Bhotia woman weaves saddlebag material on a backstrap loom. Weaving is a year-round activity, conducted by women in Bhotia, Chhetri, and Thakuri communities. The saddlebags will be made to fit cow-yak crossbreeds, sheep, and goats, which carry grain from the south and salt from the north.

A Bhotia woman gracefully spins wool. Isolated from machine-manufactured goods, the people of Humla rely on themselves for survival. Spinning wool is an addiction all share—Bhotia, Chhetri, Thakuri, young, and old. Coarse, inferior Humla *ronglu* mountain wool is spun to make blankets, while the long-fiber Tibetan *changla* sheep wool is spun and woven for clothes.

22

Backs bend in unison as women scythe fields of barley. Fall is the back-breaking season of sweat, blisters, calluses. An unspoken fear overshadows all who work. Will this harvest be as meager as the last? The shouts of bartering for sheep and grains at the traders' fair ring with the urgency of necessity: stock-piling for winter. Yet with the resilience of a mountain-bred spirit, villagers wipe away harvest dirt to celebrate the bounty of the land with festive harvest weddings.

We tromp across a field of swirling dust clouds toward a solitary farmer resting in the shade beside his yak and plow. He wipes his sweaty, soil-caked brow. He beckons our company. "In autumn the dust of the earth clings to the skin but not to the land," he says. "The fields are hungry for manure." Grateful for his plentiful supply, the old farmer worships Padme, the lotus-goddess of dung. "Dung is more valuable than gold to a hungry field," he explains.

A single-minded devotion to harvest tasks prevails. No matter how menial or difficult the chore, work is considered a sacred act of prayer. In a field nearby, a group of women stoop and scratch at the rocky soil. Uncovering ripened turnips and parsnips, they gather the roots to dry and store for winter.

Little gypsy urchins, black with soot, scamper barefoot down mountain trails with baskets of wood. At each step, they expel clouds of frozen breath into the Himalayan air. Dressed in rags, they sing under the burden of painstakingly gathered fuel.

We follow them to their destination. Shafts of smoke from roasting grains emerge from a rooftop chimney hole. A woman winnows purple beans, shaking them to the ground and blowing away the dust and chaff. Beside her, curled pumpkin strips hang from a rafter. Sitting with her granddaughter, an old woman rhythmically slices coarse turnips with her leathery hands.

Her neighbor wades through the winter supply of drying turnip chips, aerating them with her weather-beaten feet as she leaves a swirling wake of patterns behind her. In the courtyard, another woman, her forehead beaded with sweat, bundles hay with a *kukuri* knife she clenches between her teeth.

Fountains of color burst in dappled glens of birch and aspen, splashing across the bleak landscape as dried leaves crunch underfoot. With rough-hewn wooden pestles, the women crush barley in worn stone mortars. The dull, steady thump of their work pervades the mountains, reverberating in the canyons, impossible to escape. As if it were the very heartbeat of existence, the pulsating rhythm of pounding grains recalls the constant struggle that means survival.

PAGE 28

On a fall evening in Simikot, a Chhetri woman winnows buckwheat, tipping the basket to make use of the wind.

PAGE 29

Chhetri women of Simikot use two sticks to tear tips of wheat from stalks. The *chobundi* (tie-wrap jacket), bronze earrings, nose ring, glass and coin necklaces are native dress for the Chhetri women of Humla. The chobundi is styled for pregnant and breast-feeding women, who bear, in Humla, an average of six children.

PAGE 30

Jethi Aama, a widowed Chhetri grandmother, age sixty-seven, winnows chaff from her buckwheat harvest with a winnowing basket made of woven bamboo and plastered with mud. Her name means "oldest sister-mother," as she is the oldest sister (*jethi*) and now an old woman and mother (*aama*) to her younger relatives, with whom she lives. Many Hindu girls have no formal name other than one that defines their relation to other family members. Little girls are often simply called *maili, shaili, kanchi,* or *bahini* (second, third, fourth, or youngest sister) until they marry, at which time they are considered a part of Hindu society and given a formal name.

PAGE 31

Sarasoti, an exhausted but proud Chhetrini, pauses from pounding grain. In addition to beaded necklaces from trading trips in India, silver coins from British-ruled India, fashioned by *kamis*, the blacksmith caste of Humla, adorn her chest.

PAGES 32–33

Using handcrafted bamboo baskets and woven headstraps, Chhetri women carry loads of valuable compost to dump on the weary soil before the plowing and planting of winter wheat.

PAGE 34

Following her long shadow beneath a canopy of drying buckwheat stalks, a Bhotia woman carries a wooden butter churner full of water back to her home in Yakba. Single at age twenty-one, it is doubtful she will ever marry. Instead, she will continue to live in her natal home ruled by her eldest brother, helping her sister-in-law with the various female chores of a polyandrous Humla household, including fetching water, cooking meals, weeding, harvesting, and fertilizing the fields.

Discreet affairs with younger brothers in other polyandrous marriages occur frequently among single unwed women, sometimes becoming so serious that the male lover peti-

tions his brothers to bring the young woman into the polyandrous marriage. If this is agreeable to the wife, who is often in need of help with her chores, the woman is brought into the marriage as a second wife to be shared by all brothers. If the wife is not amenable or the male lover is clever and from a wealthy family he may defect from the polyandrous marriage and build separate quarters onto the family home, in which he will live with his new wife—though in much poorer conditions than he had known as part of a polyandrous arrangement.

PAGE 35

Chaff scatters to the wind as Bhotia women of Yakba winnow grain.

PAGES 36–37

With cultivatable soil scarce, houses are densely clustered to make use of all available land. In the deep snows of winter, this village arrangement allows for easy access from house to house. Late afternoon sun illuminates fluttering prayer flags and a solitary woman threshing wheat on the silhouetted rooftops of Brassi, elevation 11,700 feet.

PAGE 37

After a hard day's work in the fields, a *dhami* enjoys a smoke of harsh, home-grown tobacco from his *chillum,* a local pipe. Travelers in Humla log distance in "smokes," how far they walk in the forty-five minutes a pipeful lasts.

37

By early October herds of yaks have reluctantly descended from highland pastures, buckwheat has been cropped to shimmering stalks of copper, and the high passes have yet to see heavy snowfall. Tibetan traders from the plateau region of Limi descend with their yaks, sheep, and goats to barter for necessary goods. Huffing and puffing, Hindu Chhetri and Thakuris carry woven baskets laden with grains and butter to a high grassy basin. Tucked within a field of glacial rubble, conifers on the north ridge and a small cluster of white cotton tents on the south ridge guard the herds of highland sheep and goats. The Limi Tibetans from northern Humla camp here to trade salt, wool, goat hair, and Chinese goods for the Bhotias' and Hindus' essential provisions of butter, grains, and Indian goods.

By morning, wisps of smoke from the morning's fire waft from the Tibetan's tents. Quickly the air grows thick with the bedlam of barter and trade. As if we were on a Himalayan Wall Street, there is an underlying logic to the chaos: heated arguments require the services of a *kaba*, an arbiter who translates, checks measurements, and smooths ruffled tempers. The cries of grains, salt, wool, and butter measured cup by cup are interrupted only by the bleating pandemonium of runaway sheep and goats.

Sitting on Oriental saddle carpets, leaning against piles of bulging saddle bags, the Tibetans resemble opulent desert sheikhs. A Thakuri, with a bundle of butter wrapped in birch bark and sheepskin, approaches a Tibetan trader. The imposing Tibetan stabs it with his dagger, withdraws a sample, and grunts, "It stinks! Take it away!" The Thakuri grudgingly departs before his brother is able to strike a more reasonable deal—two meters of Indian cloth for the butter.

Dull red embers scatter across the trading basin in the rising morning mist. The yaks protest the heavy sacks of grain saddled on their backs. They kick up a dust storm, stomp and snort, steam rising from their flared nostrils. We join the caravan of traders and stubborn yaks on the five-day journey to their plateau home of Limi in northern Humla. Through a raw wilderness of conifer and rhododendron forests, glacial beds, icy mountains, frozen rivers, and a desolate desert of wind-whipped sand storms, we trustingly follow the caravan of fearless traders.

PAGES 40—41

With a surplus of harvest goods, Humla Bhotias arrive at the annual traders' fair to trade for the necessary goods of winter. Unloading sacks of grains, nuts, and butter, they will barter with Limi traders for salt, tea, *pashmina,* and Chinese goods. The once-flourishing salt and wool trade is a thing of the past. The 1959 Chinese invasion of Tibet and subsequent taxation of caravans and take-over of wheat distribution in western Tibet, as well as the eradication of malaria from the southern jungles of Nepal in the 1960s, which allowed for cheap salt from India to travel to the middle hills of Nepal, resulted in greatly diminished trade. Accordingly, Humla's traders have been forced to diversify into dealing in Thermos bottles, watches, sneakers, radios, spices, and bolts of cloth, as well as pashmina, hand-plucked hairs from the chest of the alpine goat, which is bought from Tibetan nomads and bartered for grains with the Humla traders. They, in turn, trade it with Kashmiris, who make exquisitely soft shawls from the rare hairs.

PAGE 41

Winter survival depends upon each trader's skill in striking a reasonable bargain. Centuries of distrust and resentment between Hindu Chhetris and Buddhist Bhotias erupt in trade arguments over the exchange rate of grains for salt. Though the Nepalese hold political sway in the region, the Bhotias are more prosperous. Tolerance masks the vast cultural differences (religious, social, linguistic) that prevail between the two groups scrambling to survive in an area of scarce resources.

PAGES 42—43

A Chhetri smokes a *chillum,* while watching fellow traders complete deals.

PAGE 43

The leader of the Tibetan caravan from the far northern Humla village of Limi has traveled over five days to trade *changla* sheep wool for walnuts and butter. He bargains with a Bhotia woman from the village of Yakba for nuts, a mountain delicacy.

PAGE 44

The yak caravan heads north to the village of Limi, a five-day journey through wilderness terrain. The lead yak, wearing a red tassel, pilots the caravan through a conifer forest and a narrow canyon. Ominous vertical cliffs, rumored to be the abode of evil spirits, loom above. With up to eighty kilos of grains and goods upon their backs, the yaks trudge slowly, eager for the chance to rest.

PAGE 45

The terrain between central Humla and the far northern village of Limi, located on the Tibetan plateau, is vast and varied. The yak caravan trudges through rolling sand dunes created by the sweeping plateau winds. The district of Limi consists of three villages—Halje, Til, and Jang. *Limi* means "people of the confluence," for the villages rest beside the Nying Khola River. *Nying* means heart, and the Nying Khola River Valley is considered sacred ground—Pamasambhava traveled this way on his pilgrimage to Mount Kailash.

Settled by Tibetans over eight hundred years ago, Limi shares much of its culture with Tibet but is proud to be a territory of Nepal. When the Chinese invaded Tibet in 1959, they offered Limi one thousand silver coins to become a part of Chinese Tibet. The villagers prayed to their protectress-goddess, Alchi, whose oracle told the villagers to refuse the Chinese offer. Thus Limi has retained its alliance with Nepal and receives government-subsidized Nepalese rice but must pay a tax of twenty-one rupees ($1.00) per yak for grazing in Tibet.

PAGES 46—47

Up at dawn, traders must work together to survive the bitter cold and get their animals safely home. Age and experience dictate each trader's task in keeping the caravan moving. Boys round up stubborn yaks in the freezing morning daybreak. Another trader collects yak dung left behind from herding the summer before. Yet another has to cook the tea and prepare a stew, while others break camp. Night is spent in cotton tents with Tibetan carpets and a smoking, dung-fueled stove for warmth. Once the yaks are gathered together, men pair to saddle the snorting beasts. One man on horseback oversees six yaks on the caravan.

PAGES 48—49

Fighting a vicious wind, the Limi caravan trudges around frozen glacial pools.

PAGES 50—51

The Nyalu Pass, elevation 17,300 feet. Despite the piercing cold winds at this elevation, thick sheepskin coats (*lhakpas*), keep the men warm. Once the Limi men cross this pass they reach their own territory. Their excitement is tempered with devotion. They prostrate themselves toward sacred Mt. Kailash (Khang Rimpoche), the holiest mountain in the universe for Hindus and Tibetans. It appears on the distant horizon.

PAGES 52—53

A Lone Tibetan trader stands silhouetted below the Nyalu Pass. One can often distinguish between a Limi Tibetan and a central Humla Bhotia by his braided hair with red threads wrapped around the head. The Limi men are proud of their heritage and isolation from the rest of Humla's inhabitants. The Limi men live a seminomadic life, spending over eight months of the year trading and herding. They can be found as far afield as New Delhi, India, trading for cotton and watches during the winter months. Intertwining religious and economic aims, trading trips and pilgrimages become one. It has been said that if religion is the heart of Tibetan culture, trading is surely its lungs.

PAGE 54

Limi villages are well above the treeline. A Halje villager returns from collecting dung, which will be used for cooking fuel. In a treeless environment, yak dung becomes a precious commodity. She carries her dung in a *doko*, a basket secured to the head by a strap, Changla sheep stand in the background.

PAGE 55

In a playground of stone, children congregate beside the village *chorten*, a monument erected to protect the settlement from wandering evil spirits. Chortens, "receptacles of worship," contain relics—commonly bone fragments or ashes of buddhas, bodhisattvas, or enlightened beings. The origin of these structures can be traced to the death and cremation of Buddha. Chortens thus symbolize the mind of Buddha and the means of salvation. Great spiritual merit is procured by the construction of a chorten; merit is also gained by circumambulating one. Chortens function as landmarks and trail markers. A chorten is always approached and passed on the pilgrim's right (Bonpo followers circumambulate to the left). Animals are so accustomed to this tradition that they naturally walk to the right of the structure.

41

After the harvest is reaped and supplies for winter gathered at the traders' fair, fatigue is replaced with merry-making. We eagerly partake in the festivities, opulent harvest weddings in thanksgiving for the season's gifts. Filled with drama, romance, and the splendor of legend, weddings are a form of theater in which all forget the toil of harvest and look to the future refreshed with hope.

At the monogamous Chhetri and Thakuri weddings, the "capture" of the bride is played out with dramatic flair. Her girlfriends vigorously but unsuccessfully fight off the groom's band of kidnapping Rajput sword dancers. With much bravado, the turbaned and mustachioed dancers encircle the bride, brandishing their long swords as they serenade her. In the style of classic Hindu epics, the tearful bride is carried away to live—happily ever-after—in her new home.

The polyandrous Bhotia wedding is a reenactment of the celebrated courtship of Tibet's beloved seventh-century king Songsten Gompo and the Chinese princess Wen Cheng Konjo. Replete with magnificent costumes of Chinese silk and brocade, the romantic misadventures of thirteen centuries ago come alive in an operatic sing-song between the wedding parties.

In the *dharamsala*, a structure that houses ceremonial affairs, the young bride of ten is transformed from a harvest turnip picker to a regal princess. Her face is hidden behind strands of coral and silver that taper off into raindrops, and her turquoise-studded headdress, swathed in blessing scarves, creates a royal crown above her head. Quivering with fright, she is shielded by her ornate decorations. She wears a silk-embroidered fur jacket. Enormous jewels, charm boxes, and *gaos*—portable altar boxes—hang heavily from her neck.

Amid the cacophony of cymbals, horns, drums, and the chanting of monks, the grooms' representatives enter the smoky chamber with much pomp and ceremony. Curling blue incense from branches of juniper drifts like spiderwebs through the room. After a formal high-pitched wail of welcome, the singing evolves into a sing-song debate in which each side—bride's and grooms'—tests the other's worthiness.

A bird and turtle fashioned out of barley flour are placed before the grooms' representatives. It is a riddle: "Where do these creatures live, and what do they represent?" sings the bride's side.

"One flies through the air, the other through water. The turtle holds up the universe, the bird protects life, and so this bride shall be like the turtle, the husband like the bird," the grooms' representatives eloquently reply.

Centuries earlier, brides were often kidnapped by frustrated grooms who failed such trials, a tradition of tests believed to be borrowed from the Bonpo shaman's practice of outwitting evil spirits by asking similar questions.

Rendered orator by barley beer, our friend the caravan leader recounts to us the legend on which this marriage ceremony is based:

"Long ago, King Songsten Gompo decided to win the hand of the fair Chinese princess Wen Cheng Konjo. He sent his cleverest prime minister, Longpo Dhentsen, to China to woo her.

"Wen Cheng Konjo's father, thinking that Tibetans were nothing more than barbaric nomadic yak herders, hoped to prevent Longpo Dhentsen from winning the competition by presenting Longpo with the impossible task of threading a twisted bead of turquoise without breaking it.

"Discouraged, Longpo lay in the grass as he pondered this riddle. Then, spying a trail of wandering ants, he tied a string to the leg of one and trained it to walk through the twisted turquoise hole. Longpo won the bride for his king and country."

The grooms' relatives play the role of Longpo Dhentsen by dressing in native hand-spun burgundy robes with otter and muskrat trim and pancake-style felt berets. As was the case with King Songsten Gompo, the grooms' success in winning the bride depends entirely upon the cleverness of the representatives in solving the riddle of the courtship trials.

After the riddle is answered, feasting begins with shanks of yak meat, beer, fried barley, and bread. Bellowing like hoarse yaks, swaying with drink, all raucously toast and sing of what ideal partners these grooms and this bride will make—like mortar and pestle, yak and plow, wool and spindle.

It is the oldest brother who consummates the polyandrous marriage, and he has authority over the other husbands. Shoes are discreetly left outside the wife's door as a signal to the others that it is too late for a late-night liaison.

With most brothers at any given time away on trading and herding trips, paternity is readily established. Nevertheless, polyandry is fragile, as delicate as the ecosystem that fosters it. Affairs abound, and many marriages dissolve in discord. Sometimes another woman (commonly the sister to the wife) is brought into the marriage to help with the many chores and to appease the younger brothers. More often, households split, and the younger brothers marry and build their own quarters adjacent to their brother's house. The Bhotias liken a good wife to the *kha,* or pillar that supports the house; for it is up to her to quell the eruption of tempers between often jealous, quarreling brothers. Like harvest time in Humla, polyandrous weddings require hard work and depend upon the most important element for survival in the mountains: cooperation.

PAGE 58

Chhetri wedding procession. In the tradition of their Rajput ancestors, intent on "capturing" the bride, representatives of the groom wield swords while marching to a drum. The *damais,* a caste of tailors who traditionally form makeshift bands to play religious music for weddings and other occasions, serve as drummers.

PAGE 59

Leaving behind her birthplace and childhood, a frightened Chhetri bride is veiled and whisked away to a new life in her husband's home. Life is not easy for a young Hindu bride. Though her family will have given a dowry with the marriage, her position in the new family is not an enviable one. Mothers-in-law are often suspicious of the newcomer vying for the affections of a son, and they leave to her the least desirable chores. No other person in Chhetri society is more commonly accused of practicing witchcraft than a new bride. Her status will not improve until she bears a son.

This Chhetri bride is moving only from upper Simikot (Paubara) to lower Simikot (Kaduk), whereas the Thakuris intermarry with the middle-hills Chhetris of Bajang and Bajura in the South. During winter trading/herding trips, trade relationships are established with Bajang and Bajura families and marriages arranged to strengthen these ties. Unlike Chhetri marriages, which traditionally occur after harvest, Thakuri marriages take place in April and May, when men return from the South with their brides-to-be. Thakuris maintain more orthodox Hindu customs than the Humla Chhetris due to the continual influx of Hindu women from the South.

PAGE 61

Bhotia wedding ceremony. Tea-and-beer servers await the bridal party outside the Halje village monastery. Halje, with a population of 382, is the only Sakyapa Buddhist village in Limi. Before the bride may enter her new home she must first become acquainted with the protector deities of the home and village.

PAGES 62–63

Wedding preparations inside the *dharamsala* (public resthouse used as the bride's ceremonial hall). Great concentration is needed for the task of plaiting 108 wedding-ceremony braids. Female wedding attendants use straw for brushes to apply oil to the hair. Many of these Limi girls will never have the chance to marry in this polyandrous society. Many will bear children out of wedlock.

PAGES 64–65

Like an actress caught off-stage, a wedding guest waits to receive barley beer and Tibetan salt-butter tea during the wedding ceremony. Light from the roof cutout cascades into the smoky *dharamsala*. Curling incense dances among the shadows of the finely dressed guests as a woman sips tea from a hand-carved *puro,* a wooden teacup. While the men from the groom's and bride's side sing, beer and tea are served to soothe sore throats. Smudges of butter, acting as blessings, adorn the puros. Food and drink are ceremonially tossed in the air as an offering to accompany the three-fold affirmation of refuge—"I take refuge in the Buddha, the Dharma, and the sangha!"—as guests renew their Buddhist vows. Food is symbolically offered, removed, and reoffered to the guests during the operatic ceremony. It is not until the end of the ceremony that men stuff the shanks of meat, the fried bread, and *tsampa* into their *chubas* to take home and share with their families.

PAGE 66

Heavy *gaos* hang from the ten-year-old bride's neck as she shyly peers from behind a veil of silver and coral beads. The gao is a portable shrine, altar, and charmbox used to ward off evil spirits and bring good luck. Gaos usually contain a deity, mantras, or some other sacred object. In former times, the most valued additions to a gao were nail parings from the Dalai Lama, or the hair from a high Lama's head (or a scrap of his food, or a piece of his robe). When Tibetan soldiers fought the English in 1904, they performed mad acts of bravery in the belief that their gaos would protect them.

Tibetans invest a great deal in jewelry. Displaying generations of accumulated wealth, the bride brings this inherited dowry with her to the groom's house. Wealthy wives of high-ranking officials often wear up to $20,000 worth of gems.

This arranged marriage will not be consummated until the bride reaches puberty, and until that time, she will remain in her parents' home.

PAGE 67

While Chhetri marriages are monogamous, Bhotia marriages are polyandrous. In the wedding pictured here, the shy young groom happens to be an only son; however, should brothers be born into his family, they will share the wife with him. He wears an ornate Chinese silk gown lined with sheepskin and a hat wrapped with a *khata* (blessing scarf). His dangling earring signifies his clan's prominence as high-ranking officials in the village.

In this particular wedding, the ten-year-old bride will return to her parents' house following the ceremony; there she will remain until she comes of age. Were she already mature, bride and groom would be taken after the ceremony to a private room. Under the carpet in this room is a swastika—symbol of good fortune—traced in barley flour. The couple lies together on the carpet and, legend has it, if the swastika is not obliterated by their love-making, the groom is better suited to the celibate life of a monk and the deities of the home do not welcome the bride.

PAGE 68

Attempting to persuade the bride's family of the groom's worthiness, representatives proudly sing of the groom's family's status and prestigious heritage, and what an honor it would be for the bride to become a part of this clan. Arrayed in pancake-style felt berets and maroon *chubas* lined with ermine, the groom's representatives—his male relatives—are *mukhiyas,* village officials, among whose responsibilities is familiarity with the wedding songs.

PAGE 69

Generous hospitality is the custom of the land in Tibetan culture. *"Shay, Shay"*—"drink, drink"—a hostess urges one of the groom's representatives, extending her hand in offering. Dressed in a cape of distinctive textiles from the neighboring Purang region of Tibet, she wears a shirt in the colors of the five elements that compose the Tibetan universe: blue for sky, white for clouds, red for fire, green for water, and yellow for earth.

PAGE 70

This ceremony is an operatic reenactment of the marriage of Chinese princess Wen Cheng Konjo with the seventh-century Tibetan king Songsten Gompo. Thus, one of the groom's representatives, acting the part of Longpo Dhentsen—the king's representative—leads the bride to the groom's house, singing songs of victory upon winning the bride through his cleverness and skill. Weddings give the villagers a chance to dress in silken finery and display their brocaded Chinese robes embroidered with dragons, clouds, and ocean motifs.

PAGE 71

"May your home always know abundance and never know want," the groom's female relatives sing to the bride and her delegates inside the groom's courtyard. The women offer the bride milk, barley, tea, and a *torma* (a ritual statue made of dough) as symbols of prosperity and wealth. Waving a flag on the rooftop, the groom sings "Chang chor yang chor!"—"Partner come, let us share our wealth."

The sweat of harvest labor has been wiped away,
the crumbs from wedding feasts have been swept up,
the songs of legends past are now silent.
Like confetti, snow pigeons flutter and descend from the mountains,
seeking refuge in the village.
Soon the village will be swaddled in white,
ready for the slumber of winter.

WINTER

Winter is refuge. Winter is frozen silence.
People whisper and walk on hushed tiptoe,
seeking solace beside the hearth, with each other
and alone in contemplation.
Subdued and somber, winter in the mountains
demands a kind of inward hibernation to survive the bitter cold.
Winter penetrates—to the soul of oneself
as much as to the soles of one's shoes.
Humla's winters are filled with fireside tales
of brooding darkness, superstition, and ghosts.
Winter is death, winter is peace.
Winter is vulnerability and endurance.

The mountains of Humla seem to listen to the moan and snap of a lonely branch in the howling wind of a winter night as indifferently as to the sound of a solitary monk singing prayers of petition. In return, the people listen to the mountains. They hear them roar and crack with avalanche thunder. They hear the gods of the mountains speak. Snowbound, lamas and dhamis listen with reverence, retreating to caves for a season of prayer.

Snow descends from a sky saturated with clouds, whitewashing the dreary dark soil. Harsh cliffs with tufts of gramma grass blur in the sweeping clouds of falling snow. A once-roaring waterfall is caught, suspended in air, a sculpture of contoured ice, frozen in an aquiline pallor of silence. In the far distance a little Chhetri girl, her feet cracked and bare, hands chapped and numb, carries a basket of manure to fertilize the snow-crested fields.

In the muffled silence of falling snow, villagers are drawn indoors to the warmth of blazing hearths for gossip, spinning wool, and spinning prayer wheels. Outside, a dusting of snow gathers on the cold gray cliffs, stone walls, baskets, woodpiles, and home-thrown clay water pots. The round of chores never ends: fetching water and wood, shoveling snow, herding the animals—and the occasional snowball fight.

We stay in the smoky, mud-floor home of Takha Bahadur, the most respected dhami in the Chhetri village of Simikot. He is reflective, like most men of god. Yet Takha Bahadur is plagued with restless dark spirits who haunt his home. His wife is possessed by a forgotten goddess of the valley, Bhavani, who shouts that she is ignored, that she must be made offerings of honey and milk. "The goddess is acting up again," he says, shaking his head. We decide it is best to move on.

PAGE 74

Snow clouds threaten a grazing Himalayan pony above the village of lower Simikot (Kaduk). The highly prized animals are used primarily for rounding up the sheep and goats on trading trips.

in freshly fallen snow.

PAGE 80

The deified Changla Mountain peak, shrouded in mist, looms above the Nyinba Valley and Dozom River.

PAGE 81

Mountains meet above the village of Yakba.

PAGE 82

Simikot villagers bring home bundles of wood

chopped with kukuri knives and hatchets in the forests above. Unlike most of Nepal, which suffers from severe deforestation, Humla's sparsely populated mountains (twenty-five persons per square mile) still abound in trees. Yet this abundance of wood makes the carrying chore no less difficult or tiresome. Singing, women carry the wood with a hemp rope resting on their forehead.

PAGE 83

Like most survival chores, gathering wood is not an occupation for the Chhetris alone. Ang Dolma, a fifteen-year-old Bhotia from the village of Dhiga, returns from a day of herding dzopkios (cow-yak crossbreeds) with a bundle of wood slung on her back. She wears a choowa, the native Bhotia dress of Humla.

PAGES 84–85

As the fields lie slumbering, building activities increase in the winter months. A Chhetri villager hauls cut lumber from the forest to

build a government building in Simikot. Cash is scarce in a barter economy, and the wages for government construction work high. Paid the equivalent of two dollars a day, this man feels fortunate for the opportunity to work. Most of his wages will be used to buy rice and cloth.

PAGE 85

In winter, keeping clean comes second to keeping warm. Nevertheless, a Chhetri girl braves the cold of the dhara (the water spring) to wash clothes. She gathers kindling, heats water in a brass pot, and kneads the clothes clean with her bare feet, using ground-root.

PAGES 86–87

Man and animal must bear the elements together. A Bhotia man herds his horses through a stubble field in the village of Bargaon. Wrapped in a lhakpa, a sheepskin jacket, and wearing glasses that shimmer like nickels in the cold, the herder will take the horses up to the high pastures for grazing.

soap. In warmer months the dhara is crowded with bathing women and gossip.

PAGE 88

Special bonds of friendship are created between man and animal in the mountains, particularly among the *lattos* (cretins), who make up a large portion of the herders. Ringin spends more time with his prized white yak Karma in the high pastures than he does with villagers. (White yaks are rare; *Karma* means "star" in the Tibetan language.) The lack of iodine in Humla's diet results in a high incidence of goiter, and women with goiter have a greater chance of giving birth to retarded children. In contrast to the ostracization the retarded suffer in modern culture, cretins are fully integrated members of the family in Humla.

PAGE 89

A cretin from the Bhotia village of Bargaon trudges up the trail with a *doko*, carrying water from the *dhara*. He wears *tsoompas*, gladiator-like shoes made from hemp rope. Until 1927, when Chandra Shumshere J. B. Rana abolished slavery, Bhotias of the Nyinba Valley of Humla owned slaves. Though descendants of slaves are now free by law, the class-conscious Bhotias do not consider them to be "of good bone." Descendants of slaves tend to intermarry among themselves, struggling to survive on small land plots, while former land owners retain power and prestige.

PAGES 90–91

After heavy snows, flat mud-packed roofs must be quickly cleared to prevent damage. Each house is equipped with hand-carved wooden snow shovels. Most Bhotia marriages in Humla are polyandrous, but Nyeema is the second wife in a polygamous marriage to Karmo, a relatively prosperous land owner in the village of Bargaon. His first wife was barren, so he marred Nyeema, who shovels snow with her daughter Tsing Puti and son Kangri. After the birth of Kangri, Nyeema has been unable to conceive another child. "Man is like the farmer," Karmo told us. "I have sown seed in my wife, yet no child grows." Doctors believe the apricot-seed oil used in Humla for cooking compromises male fertility. In an economy dependent upon many hands, children are crucial to economic success and to security in old age.

PAGES 92–93

Bhotia children from the village of Yakba romp in a rooftop game of "chicken," attempting to off-balance the others while bouncing in the air. Imagination and culture help to shape the form of play among children in the barren mountains of Humla. Small looms are made as toys for little girls; little boys make slingshots and bows and arrows out of supple birch branches. Stones serve as marbles. A stick draws hopscotch squares in the dirt, and adult ceremonies are endlessly mimicked. Children play *dhami*, pretending to shake as if possessed. Blowing a conch horn and burning a fake corpse, the children stage a mock funeral. Others beat drums and wield swords, playing wedding. But none of the Chhetri girls wants to play the frightened bride. Instead, they vie for the coveted role of mother-in-law; for it is she who has the prestige and power.

In such a hostile environment, child mortality is high, especially among Bhotia girls. In a culture with a tradition of polyandry, female infanticide occurs through the sanctioned practice of neglect. Female children are the last to be fed in the family and are often the least well-dressed during the harsh winter months.

PAGE 94

Bundled against the cold, a Chhetri mother and daughter endure the bitter cold. Exposure to the cold and cooking with fire have numbed the hands of these hardy mountain women, some of whom still go barefoot in the dead of winter.

PAGE 95

Uncut hair wrapped in a white turban, and dangling brass earrings distinguish the *pujari* as a man of god. Wise and articulate, the pujari assists the *dhami*. He must be well versed in the history and lore of the region. When the dhami enters a trance, the pujari mediates between the supplicant villager and the god who possesses the dhami. It is the pujari who offers the sacrifice to the gods. The pujari is with his grandchildren.

PAGES 96–97

Takka Bahadur Rokaya, age forty-two, is the most respected of all *dhamis* in Simikot. He received the call at twenty-one from the local lineage deity, Kalo Silto: "I awoke in a shaking house, it was as if an earthquake had struck, then I began to tremble. A warm glow pervaded my body. I knew that I had been chosen by the gods. I then went to Lake Manaswarvor [a sacred lake created by the "tears" of snow from Mt. Kailash, considered the navel of the universe by Hindus and Buddhists]. Like other dhamis, I took a purification bath and vowed never to cut the hair growing from the top of my head. At my initiation ceremony, the villagers gave me gold earrings, silver bracelets, and white cloth for a turban to keep my sacred locks stored until ceremony time."

Takha Bahadur Rokaya wears the *daura surwal*, the traditional suit for men throughout Nepal. Like his ancestors from Rajasthan, he wears a turban. On his feet are *tsoompas*, footwear borrowed from the Humla Bhotias; on his forehead, a *tika*, vermilion powder that signifies his having performed morning communion with the gods. Smoking his *chillum*, Takha Bahadur reflects upon the condition of his possessed wife.

PAGE 98

Scherzoom, mother of six, cooks *puri* (a special treat of fried wheat dough) for visiting relatives. The hearth, communal center of the home and family, is strictly the domain of the wife. It is here that family politics surface. If the woman of the house is displeased with a member of the family, she will show her displeasure in the size of portions given at meal time. This is not the only means by which a wife may display her feelings near the hearth. In Bhotia homes, the seat beside the pillar, or *kha*, which supports the structure, is reserved for the head of the household or the most prestigious guest. Each succeeding position holds less rank. Although her husband has final authority in determining who sits where, the wife may also indicate, through gesture, where a guest should sit. In Bhotia society, a good wife is herself identified with the kha—for she is the support of the family— and the word *kha* is actually used to describe her. Moreover, while male family members propitiate *pho-las* (lineage-clan protector deities), women, when they marry, are first introduced to the home's hearth goddess, whose abode is the kha. The goddess is angered if anything is spilled into the fire.

Scherzoom has borne fourteen children, of whom the first nine died in infancy. She attributes their deaths to a neighbor witch.

PAGE 99

Dorje, Scherzoom's grandson, eyes his grandmother's *puri* treat.

94

Snowflakes disappear into the gray clouds of mist in the small canyon village of Yakba. The eerie, Japanese-like ridges and cliffs appear above and disappear, vanishing in the sweeping mist. We seek refuge with our good friends Eppi and Lobsong, with whom we have shared the seasons. Over time, we have developed a special rapport with them. At their request, we have placed their grandchildren in school in Kathmandu, where we look after them.

Eppi and Lobsong live in a carved cave hermitage, a tumble-down structure of boulders and scorched beams tucked against the outcroppings of a cliff. Eppi, whose name simply means "grandma," has lived with her husband, Lobsong, whose name means "Blessed one," for over sixty years. Lobsong is a lama, a Buddhist monk of the Nyingmapa sect, the oldest in Tibetan Buddhism, which allows monks to marry.

Overjoyed to see us, Eppi takes us by the hand and leads us inside to the warmth of the fire. She sits in her position as eternal tender of the hearth, swinging her heavy mani wheels with texts hidden inside as she chants mantras, counting them with her mani necklace. "*Om mani padme hum*" (Hail, jewel in the heart of the lotus!), she whispers—a sound so prevalent on the lips of every Bhotia in winter.

Lobsong treats Tom like a grandson. Through the seasons they have spent hours meditating together in Lobsong's sanctuary. I stay with Eppi, near the hearth, fighting the chill that never leaves. I help Eppi, when I can—not that she needs any help. Drawn to the notion of work, she seems to relish tasks like a life force. Chopping wood, feeding the animals, stirring broth, making tea, or tearing dried yak shanks are all met with an equal, unfailing grace. Eppi blows on the red embers, her sunken skin stretched across her cheekbones; her cheeks, like bellows, persuading the flames to leap higher into the air. Unlike in the village, where all houses are connected by windows to pass gossip for entertainment and embers for fire, in the hermitage Eppi must bury live coals and keep a vigilant eye on the ashes.

Her face resembles a walnut, her work-worn skin the bark of a majestic oak, her ageless eyes sparkle like black sapphires—aware and all-seeing. Lama, the contemplative one, looks more like a squirrel in his old age—or a cat, really, his almond eyes deeply sunk.

Lobsong's skin is not as tough as Eppi's. It is more like delicate parchment, like the yellowed texts he chants at night. Eppi's eyes sparkle with the light of compassion, Lobsong's with the light of wisdom. But Lobsong is old and sick. As winter progresses, the pallor of death overtakes him. Fragile and weak, he consults the Tibetan astrological calendar and calmly tells us, "I will die in five days. It is an auspicious day to die."

Lobsong Lama, in lotus position, holds a *drilbu* and *dorge*, ritual accoutrements used in meditation. The dorge, called the thunderbolt or diamond scepter, is unique to Tibetan Buddhism. It is believed to have originated in the fertilizing lightning bolt of the male sky gods. It is a symbol of male energy, incredible power, the absolute and suggests the immutable, awakened, empty self and the skillful exercise of wisdom. The drilbu, or bell, symbolizes the wisdom exercised by the dorge, a wisdom of openness that uses the circumstances of the moment to determine its expression. The drilbu, female counterpart of the dorge, also stands for impermanence; its sound dies away, perceived but not retained. The drilbu and dorge drive away evil.

PAGES 103–9

Lobsong and Eppi. Lobsong was born in Kham, a region in eastern Tibet. Khampas are tall fierce people, known as bandits and brave warriors since the time of Marco Polo. But Lobsong became a lama and studied in the great Tibetan university-monastery of Ganden, once the third largest in the world. As Lobsong's guru lay dying, he asked Lobsong to marry his wife, Eppi, and care for her. Lobsong did, and the couple set out together in 1951 on a pilgrimage to the holiest mountain in Asia, Mt. Kailash—Khang Rinpoche, as it is called in Tibetan. At this time they heard that the Chinese had invaded Kham. A divination was thrown, which told them there was no hope of return to Tibet.

As they made their way to India, they stopped in the small Humla village of Yakba—a mere five days' walk from Khangrimpoche. The villagers requested that Lobsong stay and perform the necessary rituals to pacify the hungry ghosts who lived above the village. Lobsong relented, and he and Eppi built a hermitage into the cliff wall where the villagers feared to tread.

Lobsong rose daily before dawn and with his dorge and drilbu made prayers and offerings, particularly the *cho puja*, in which the lama offers up his entire body to appease the hungry ghosts. Frequently he visited the village to perform ceremonies for death, illness, prosperity, long life, or weddings. Sometimes the villagers consult the lama, asking him to throw a *sho mo*, a divination using prayer beads, dice, and the consultation of texts to determine the significance of the roll.

Lobsong was a special man. Contrary to tradition, even Hindus occasionally sought him for his wisdom. Gorkha, the son of Hindu *dhami* Takha Bahadur came and asked: "Lama, my mother is crazy—possessed. What can be done about her bouts of insanity?" Lama threw a sho mo and, without having met the woman, made a diagnosis. "Your mother is possessed by a *naga* [primeval snake god] dwelling in a dried water source behind your house, marked by a white stone. The naga is angry because people on the trail are relieving themselves on the rock. If you do proper *puja* and persuade people to urinate elsewhere, the naga will no longer possess your mother." It wasn't until a full year later that Gorkha's father, the dhami, came to the same conclusion concerning his wife's bouts with insanity.

While Lobsong was known and loved for his wisdom, Eppi is loved for her sheer compassion. She is in constant motion, every action infused with prayer and devotion. Beside the hearth, Eppi twirls her *manichorkor*, a device that spins a full prayer skyward to heaven with every revolution. Lobsong meditates by the light of *lutoks*, pitch-pine wood from which turpentine is extracted.

Descending home to the villages,
we find a snowstorm has smothered
an overeager early plum-blossom tree.
A herder, his eyeglasses shimmering
like frosted nickels in the cold,
leads his horses across a stubble field.
This morning, a flock of snow pigeons,
in dazzling clouds of flickering white wings,
disappeared into the mountain skies.
Tokens of spring.

SPRING

The ground and air ring with an unforgiving cold.
Spring still seems a distant dream.
But mere whispers of soft breezes caress the sleeping fields.
Hints of pale green emerge across the barren landscape.
And the rumor of renewal
travels through the mountains like wildfire.

PAGES 120–21

On the first day of spring, fertile Chhetri women will gather for *Chitaloe,* a festival reminiscent of the European Maypole rites. Dancing and singing in robes of saffron and gold, they will circle the village pole (home of the local deity), urging the bleak brown ground to wake and bear fertile crops.

PAGES 124–25

Bhotia children delight in spring's gift, fragrant peach blossoms.

PAGE 126

The Buddhist *dhami* from the Bhotia village of Brassi sits beside the small Gura temple, looking south. Spring comes to the villages, leaving the snow-covered Saipal range untouched. An ancient blood-thirsty god from the South, Gura demands a spring goat sacrifice to ensure bountiful fields. Gura speaks through the entranced Buddhist dhami and gives villagers advice on what days to till, plant, and sow.

PAGE 127

The wealthy horseshoe-shaped Bhotia village of Bargaon. At 9,700 feet, Bargaon is rich with terraced fields that overlook an endless ocean of misty blue mountains. Far below, the Karnali River, Humla's main drainage, carves its way south through the Takh and Dharma ranges. Following the river's cut in the mountains eight hundred centuries ago, the Hindus' Chhetri and Thakuri ancestors migrated into Humla's valleys from the flat southern plains of India. Settling in the valleys and lowlands, the Hindus left the high mountains for the Buddhist Bhotias to settle.

PAGES 128–29

Spring planting. With a pair of yoked *dzos* and a wooden plow, Nomgyal breaks up the sod to till and plant *palpur,* sour yellow buckwheat, in a field beside the Bhotia village of Brassi. The villagers work with the plow used in Greece five thousand years ago. The wooden tips may break several times a day, but farmers refuse to use iron-tipped plows, claiming the animals would not be able to drag such plows through the soil.

PAGES 130–31

After the hibernation of winter, the vast expanse of the outdoors is welcomed by such diverse activities as weaving and herding horses to the high pastures.

PAGE 132

Spring is a chance to gossip and wash. Eppi is groomed while catching up on recent gossip.

PAGE 133

With a pestle older and larger than herself, Tsing Puti pounds root for shampoo. After washing, her hair will be greased with mustard oil for the Bhotia spring solstice festival, Mani.

PAGE 134

The Buddhist Mani festival has its rewards for

the *damais,* Chhetri tailors from the neighboring Hindu villages, who are kept busy making festive new clothes and costumes from Indian cloth.

PAGE 135

A little Chhetrini dresses for the festival in a traditional premarital white dress and shawl. Cowry shells from the Bay of Bengal are woven into her French braid, and an Indian coin necklace dangles from her neck. At one time, cowry shells were the standard currency of Humla.

PAGES 136–37

Jampal, the Buddhist *dhami* of Bargaon, uncoils his locks for a ritual purification bath prior to the ceremony. No Mani may begin without first appeasing the gods. Jampal was twenty-five years old when the god Ilsa first came to him in a dream. "He is big, white, full of light, with white wool hair," Jampal explains. Three years later, as he watched the full-moon *mela* (celebration), his heart began to tremble. Ilsa had returned. Jampal journeyed to Lake Manaswarvar, to cleanse himself and dedicate his life to Ilsa. The villagers cooked oil until it boiled, then poured it into a brass bell and conch shell, the instruments of the dhami. "If the god doesn't come to you, the oil will burn your throat," he explains. "But if the god comes to you, the oil feels like cool water." Having passed the test, Jampal received the silver bracelets and gold earrings symbolic of his new role as dhami. From that day on, he has never cut the hair from the crown of his head, the seat of sacred energies. For dramatic effect he stuffs his braid with black sheep wool before wrapping it with a silver coil.

Entranced as the god Mahakala possesses him, Manglay, the other dhami of Bargaon, dances to the hypnotic drum beats. Unlike the Buddhist dhamis of Brassi and Yakba, the dhamis of Bargaon do not sacrifice live animals. Instead, *torma* figures and milk are symbolic substitutes.

PAGE 138—CLOCKWISE FROM TOP LEFT

A Chhetrini of the *Kami* caste—the blacksmith and jeweler caste of Humla—pauses from planting turnips in a field near Simikot. Since the Kamis work so closely with fire, they are associated with the ancient Hindu fire god *Agni*—and feared for possible occult powers acquired from such an association.

Old man Bulla, the widower of Yakba. White beads of bone hang from his neck. Bulla is gifted in divination; counting his white beads he is able to decipher the gods' answers to prayers and questions.

The old Lama from Latok. When asked why he had a topknot and Hindus don't, he replied, "We [devout Buddhists] won't cut our hair until the sun melts the boulders!" He wears a *chuba,* traditional Tibetan-style robe, tied with a tie-dyed sash.

Namgyal, the wizard of Brassi. He wears a Dalai Lama pendant as a form of protection, surrounded by fake turquoise, coral, and zee stones, whose patterns are said to have been created thousands of years ago by lightning bugs in mud. Real zee stones can cost as much as three thousand dollars and are the most precious heirloom a family can possess. The stones protect against "the dragon's

roar"—thunder and lightning—which may cause one to be swallowed up by the earth.

Nomdyol, Eppi's twelve-year-old granddaughter. As the nights warm in spring, Bhotia teenagers sneak out to dance and sing under the light of the moon. Premarital sex is an accepted part of Bhotia folk courtship rituals. Bhotias have no word in their language for "romantic love." Undue attachment and sentiment toward another is considered *dodchag,* a vice thought to produce mental suffering. Love is considered socially disruptive, because it creates attachment to this world and interferes with the pursuit of salvation. Not that this ideal prevents affairs of the heart.

In chimneyless homes, the villagers burn pine, which coats everything with oily soot. One man told us, "When winter snow turns white, the people turn black." A nose ring and fiery spirit are all that glow in the unwashed face of a flirtatious Chhetrini down at the *dhara,* ready to wash away winter's grime.

PAGE 139

Brother and sister Kangri and Tsing Puti clown with a Mani mask made from an animal head. Kangri and Tsing Puti are from the Bhotia village of Bargaon, which, with the villages of Limitang, Torpu, Brassi, and Latok, is home to the Nyinbas—"people of the sunny valley." A distinct ethnic group with a strong sense of identity, Nyinbas have their own unique dialect and singular style of dress; they rarely marry Bhotias. With a current population of approximately 1,300, the Nyinbas trace their ancestors' migrations to Humla from western Tibet and consider themselves culturally Tibetan.

126

131

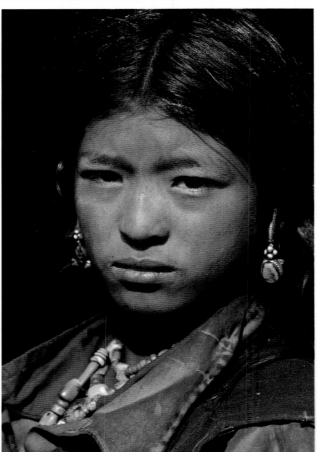

The spirit of spring is in the air, spreading impatiently. The weary coat of winter is gleefully cast aside in exuberance and reverie. Nature is giddy for the babe of all seasons, ready to laugh and chatter, explode in a shower of snow-dusted petals from the spring plum tree, "a tree of laughter and talk," the Japanese poet Basho called it.

Spring breeds giggles, gossip, and silliness. It is a time for renewal, the retying of old ties and the budding of new romance. The ice melts, and movement again begins on the trails. Families jubilantly come together as sheep caravans return from the South, laden with grains. Wooden plows are dusted and mended in preparation for breaking the cranky winter soil. Fields will soon be sown with buckwheat, turnips, and amaranth.

The essence of the season is manifested in Mani, a three-day theatrical performance celebrating the rite of spring. Each Bhotia village has its own Mani celebration with its own style and tradition. It is simply entertainment to celebrate being, to express the inexpressible through shared laughter.

In a splash of color and festivity, the villagers primp, bathing neglected winter skin. Tugging at snarled locks, plucking stubborn lice, all liberally douse their tawny skin with mustard oil, to make themselves shine like gods in the alpine sun. Heirlooms are scrubbed; the best clothes drawn from locked chests. Villagers prepare to shake off what remains of cabin fever with the biggest festival of the year. Like an Asian Mardi Gras, Mani is audacious, outrageous, and blossoming with robust bad taste.

The cold melts in giggles of outrageous mockery as the town jester, in Far Eastern vaudeville, attacks every institution and belief held sacred. Clothes are worn backward and inside out, village elders are satirized in a parody of religious life, and youths are allowed to stay out all night carousing in reckless abandon. The world is brand new and topsy turvy. Creativity surges, and spontaneous theater flourishes like an alpine weed in the rock and stubble. Tom and I are not immune to the mockery and provide ample material for amusement. The town joker picks up a rock for a camera and starts to snap and click at Tom, much to the roaring delight of the crowd.

Mani is a chance to transcend the mundane in elaborate costumes. While winter brings sober reflection on mortality, spring brings glorious hope: the possibility that one might not merely mimic but actually become one with the gods. Mani tells the universal drama of the triumph of good over evil. The Bhotias reenact the settling of the village, which, with the help of ancestor deities, involved the vanquishment of local demons who kidnap women and children.

Flirtation is the rule. Diverging paths are littered with mysterious scraps of lovers' cloth—signs of witchcraft, as men and women resort to love potions and amulets in the art of bewitching and bewildering.

Humor erupts and perversity prevails in bawdy drama, as the village is transformed into a grand stage, with every villager a performer. Men dress in drag for a cheap laugh. Drink flows to excess and spirits melt into one bacchanal.

With masks and heads pointed toward the sky, dancers bend in unison before springing upward, brandishing upraised sticks, gyrating seductively, twisting hips to the sound of the drum and the shimmering cymbal. In a Mani ballet, a masked dancer leaps into the air, his rainbow gown dazzling the crowd.

The dancers eloquently prance around the communal prayer flag. With a tug and a boom, the flagpole falls down like the descending ball at Times Square on New Year's Eve, likewise signifying the end of one year and the beginning of the next. Dhamis swirl, twisting and shaking, possessed. The dhami forcefully swings his sacred coiled braid above his head like a lasso wielded by some demented cowboy. The new pole in place, time restored, and the soul of the community centered, the frenzy cools.

By afternoon, the village is filled with the reverberating beats of the goat-hide drum,
summoning the villagers, performers, and gods
to partake in the Mani festival.

PAGE 143

A masked demon performer hides in the
shadows of the doorway, alerted by the drum
beats that Mani has begun. Families carve and
create their own masks for Mani. Parts are
given to the most talented dancers and singers,
though certain masks, associated with family
clan gods, are the possession of that particular
family. Each Mani celebration in each village
has its particular traditions unique to that
village. Even the date of the festival varies with
each village.

PAGE 144

The masked dances are not diversion but a
long-established part of Bonpo religious ceremonies. Dance is a means by which supernatural forces can be brought down to the world
of man. Dance recalls a time when the
distance between men and spirits was small.
   A young Limitang spectator watches Mani.
She wears a recently woven shawl and an
amulet to ward away evil and illness. Amulets
are often tied with astrological calculations. The
proper amulet can rescue a married couple
whose charts do not match.

PAGE 145—CLOCKWISE FROM TOP LEFT

All manifestations of human emotion are
presented at Mani: a sad-sack mask with yak-
fur beard and hair.

"Laughter draws us close together in intimacy
because our egos are dissolved. The ego shell
falls off in the laugh," writes Katsuki Sekida.
Mani is a time for laughter. Wearing a textile
from the nearby region of Purang, Tibet, a
clown shakes cowbells strung across his chest.

A masked demon, wearing torn clothes and a
sheepskin jacket turned inside out, bears a
staff and glares between performances.
Besides the entertainment the masked demons
provide, their presence serves a religious function. Spectators become acquainted with the
demonic appearance, which helps prepare
them for *bardo*, the intermediate state between
life and death during which the demons will
appear. To the villagers these demons exist and
are very real. To the high lamas, they are manifestations of consciousness—projections of
fear.

Brassi's Mahakala, wearing a *dharma* crown
and baring his vicious fangs, protects the
villagers from the demons' return. Villagers
attribute Humla's high infant mortality rate to
demons and witches. If the village fails to
perform Mani, it is believed the demons will
return to take the lives of more children.

Mani clown.

The famous Buddhist protector deity Mahakala,
carrying a shield and wielding a sword, fights
the *nagas* (or "*klus*" in Tibetan language—
serpent spirits) in a triumphant drama of good
over evil in the village of Bargaon. Mahakala
is the most important *dharmapala* (*chokyong*
in Tibetan language—protector of the faith) in

Tibetan Buddhism. Mahakala is a form of the
Hindu Shiva. Known as Gonpo in Tibetan,
Mahakala is also the protector of the tent.

PAGES 146—47

A masked performer leaps in the air in a Mani
ballet as amused spectators, wearing their
newly woven blankets, giggle in amusement.
Man is no more than the temporary dwelling
place of a divine presence to whom he lends
his body so that the god might repeat his
wonders. The performer does not actually
become the god he portrays, but rather the
god's instrument for good and evil.

PAGES 148—49

Boys, proud of the chance to participate in
Mani, dress as demons and hold staffs to
protect the village. Belief has it that the masked
demon dancers frighten away the real demons.

PAGE 150

Ghostlike death dancers, wearing skull masks
and cowry-shell belts, dramatically emerge
to the beat of the drum and the clash of the
cymbal to frighten the crowd.

PAGE 151

Bonds of tradition link old and young in a Mani
dance at Limitang village.

PAGE 153

Masked boys dangle from the best seat in
town.

From treetop vantage points, boys mock and leer,
someday hoping to play the coveted roles and be the stars of Mani.
Donning wacky masks, an aspiring troupe of Mani performers
protects the village from evil demons.
Then Mani abruptly subsides like a descending plum blossom,
as if to show that spring is as brief as any burst of laughter.

SUMMER

Lazy summer, when life is as slow as a cow chewing its cud.
In this season of well-deserved yawns,
the sky becomes a ceiling,
a boulder a pillow, the grass a downy bed.
Even the moon lies lumpish in the sky.
Summer is rich as honey dripping from a hive.
Long summer days begin with udders squeezed
and the squirt of milk against wooden bucket bottoms.
Steaming fresh buttermilk gulped from the bucket dribbles down chins,
to be wiped away with a grin.

Summer is movement and herding. Not harried, as when traders scurry home before the passes are full of snow, but slow and easy, the pace of a Sunday stroll. Summer is the sound of a ballad along a meandering trail, hummed while distractedly swatting the rear of a goat. Katydids and crickets sing to the moon. Transformed to a steamy green, village buckwheat fields no longer whisper, they burst into song.

Summer sends the folks of Humla up into the mountains. The flow of movement is mostly upward, to expansive highland pastures and summer settlements. Trails are jammed with trading and herding caravans. Only the old and the indigent stay behind to care for the villages.

Morning mist rises, and the early air is still cool. Beside the village an old woman tends to her dewy patch of wheat. She plucks the strangling weeds that invade her ripening crop. We follow her home and sit on her porch. Her face is like a dried apple, every crevice the trace of hard-won, home-grown wisdom. In the mountains, the body seems to grow older, but the spirit younger. She tells us that a grazing sheep in heaven scratches heaven's floor, causing turquoise to tumble to the ground. Precious heirloom zee stones are worn to protect against thunder and lightning—the "dragon's roar." They were made thousands of years ago by lightning bugs dancing in the mud.

As if spinning the soft summer clouds of those celestial sheep into strands of wool, she yawns and twirls her spindle with a dexterity that comes only from many a season watching the stars of summer slowly awake to light the evening sky. We fall asleep outside on her roof, our bellies full of her noodle soup and our ears full of her melodic chants.

Moving on the trails behind a sheep caravan, we find ourselves in the chaos of a mountain traffic jam as we confront a yak caravan loaded with lumber headed toward treeless Tibet. Stumbling on the trail before dawn, glazed with sweat, we stop to rest in the potent heat of the midday sun. Goats and sheep are unpacked and buckwheat pancakes set to fry on the griddle.

PAGES 156–57

A balmy morning begins with morning smoke rising above Simikot.

PAGE 160

Chhetri children from the village of Simikot watch a rainbow light up a stormy summer sky. Nepali folk-art collector Judy Chase has surmised that the abundance of summer rainbows in Humla have influenced the design motifs on the bright Mani and wedding gowns.

PAGE 161

Sumitra, a Chhetri mother, holds her first-born. The average woman in Nepal gives birth to eight children, of whom six live to adulthood.

PAGE 162

Summer is a time to daydream: three Chhetri brothers wearing *topis*, native Nepali hats, rest on a blanket beside harvested buckwheat.

PAGE 163

Chhetri sisters and relatives wear brass earrings, beads, and coin necklaces from India. Humla fashion is pragmatic: women wear *chobundi* shirts, designed for breast-feeding.

PAGE 164

Torpu Eppi. Every line in her work-worn face tells a story. In the mountains, age is a sign of wisdom in the art of survival. Torpu Eppi wears heirloom necklaces of coral, amber, and turquoise, all acquired on trading trips to Tibet.

PAGE 165

In summer craftsmen busy themselves making wooden tea cups, clay ovens, and *tozoms*, wooden butter churners, to take on trading trips north to Tibet. Pemba of Kangalgaon creates a *gokpur*, a fine wooden bowl made from the knot of a tree. Using an ingenious foot-powered lathe, he burnishes the bowl by rubbing it with boiled sheepskin sprinkled with ground glass. He will sell the *gokpurs* in Tibet for 170 rupees each—about $8.20.

PAGE 166

Old grinding stones and a swollen glacial river surround a water mill near Yakba. Husks of ground grain and straw thatch the roof of the small stone millhouse. Many small mills dot the Humla Karnali tributaries, their upkeep supported by village taxes. All who pay are allowed to use them.

PAGE 167

Husband and wife, wearing old clothes for the dusty task, grind barley before carrying the flour back home in *dzo*-hide sacks.

160

High in the pastures, only the sound of clanking yak bells penetrates the morning mist. Sauntering through the fields of red poppies dripping with the morning dew, yaks stare dully, chewing cud. In summer, children sleep outside naked under the stars, huddled underneath yak blankets only to be awakened by slobbering licks of an impatient long-lashed calf ready to play. After milking, the herders toss rocks at the herd, urging them forward. With whistles piercing the mist, they disappear into the pastures.

By noon, folks stretch out, making themselves at home in fields of wildflowers. With a hoot and a holler, children race off to the glacial streams to splash naked in the milky jade waters. Women rest in the shade of yak wool tents, plucking deerskins, churning butter, swatting flies, and drying cheese. Old men sand *tozoms* (butter churners) with ground glass glued to rawhide and carve tree knots with foot-powered lathes to make wooden teacups and bowls.

Tom spends time with ten-year-old Dawa and his grandfather Lobsong, herding sheep. Dawa is forever disappearing with his friends. One day Tom asks him, "Where do you go, Dawa?" Shy and hesitant, he finally blurts out his secret: "My friends and I lie in the deep grass and imagine the sheep getting really fat. We dream of finding *shambhala*"—a hidden valley of paradise, an earthly realm of heaven—"with lush pastures so thick the sheep may wallow in hap-piness, their coats growing thick and glossy by the moment."

If the upper pastures are not shambhala, they do at least resemble it. Shimmering silver rivers snake through the flat emerald beds dotted with grazing sheep, scree, and yak-wool tents. The rolling pastures, lush malachite green speckled with mica stones that sparkle like crushed diamonds, are guarded by the jagged cathedral-spire snow peaks that disappear into a lapis-lazuli sky.

A buxom Tibetan shepherdess with apple cheeks gamely ties her herd of balking sheep together by the horns. She drags the reluctant interlocked beasts to the steaming hot springs and, with the ease of experience, heartily swings them in the air before submerging each of the gasping flock in the hot water to cleanse their manured fleece.

By dusk, Lobsong erects a prayer flag beside his stone herding hut. Overlooking a sea of endless clouds, the long strips of cotton printed with scripture and impressions of a horse flutter with every puff of evening breeze, catching the wind like a sail. The prayer flag is called a *lungta*, which means "windhorse." Lobsong explains to us that "The windhorse transports the wisdom of the scripture printed on the flag. The wind carries the wisdom to the birds, the slugs, the snails, and all living beings in order to awaken them from the sleep of suffering."

PAGE 170

Chosa basin.

PAGE 171

Headed for pasture.

PAGE 172

Melting mountain snow creates meandering glacial streams in the Chosa Valley basin, ideal for grazing animals. A summer settlement of stone herding huts dots the foot of the mountain. Women spin, salt animal skins, milk cows, make yogurt, and dry cheese into hardened chips called *chirpi*. An ideal trail food, chirpi is also added to winter stews. Caravans of sheep wander through the valley, heading north on trading trips. No laws govern these grazing grounds, yet villagers respect the rights of those who come first.

PAGE 173

Barefoot Bhotia shepherds and shepherdesses herd a flock of *dzopkios* out to pasture. An adult *dzomo*, a female half-yak, half-cow that produces milk, is bought for the equivalent of $125.00. A *dzo*, an adult male used as a pack animal, costs $150.00. A yak costs $400.00, and a six-month-old *dzopkio*, female offspring of a yak and bull used for ploughing, costs only $100.00.

PAGE 174

Bhotia women, wearing *choowas,* native Humla Bhotia dress, scramble through the boulder-strewn terrain. With children riding papoose-style on their backs, they descend to the villages for more supplies to bring back to the summer herding settlements.

PAGE 175

Shadows sweep across the Chosa basin as the pyramid mountain, believed to be the abode of evil spirits, looms ominously above. The Himalayas are a young mountain range—only four million years old and still moving upward at the remarkable rate of several inches a year.

PAGE 176

A sheep caravan returns from Tibet with saddle bags of salt. Thirty years ago one bag of rice was traded for six bags of salt. Now one bag of rice is traded for only two bags of salt; one kilo of rice is traded for one kilo of wool; three kilos of wheat are traded for one kilo of wool. The caravan takes thirty days to travel from Simikot to Limi and back. The sheep carry twelve kilos of rice each. Though the *changla* sheep is known for its superior long-fiber wool, it is the native *ronglu* sheep that lead the caravans in the highlands; they are better at negotiating treacherous passes. In addition, the ronglu sheep are bred to endure the hotter climate of the middle hills; the prized changla sheep survive only at high altitudes.

PAGE 177

Leather sacks full of salt lay unpacked behind Bhotia salt traders relaxing for a mid-day meal. On the trail since five o'clock in the morning, the traders stop at eleven to eat and rest during the hottest part of the day. Many hours are spent playing mahjong to relieve the boredom.

PAGES 178—81

Yaks laden with lumber descend the Nyalu Pass enroute to wood-scarce Tibet. The journey will take them five long days. The lumber will be used to reconstruct a monastery destroyed during the Cultural Revolution.

PAGE 182

A Limi shepherd guides his huge flock of sheep across a small wooden bridge spanning a stream in the highlands. Shepherds pray to the *phyugs lhas pon bdon,* the "gods of the flocks."

PAGE 183

Steam rises from hot springs in the Taksi basin. Sheep are plunged into hot-spring pools to clean their manured fleece.

PAGES 184—85

Raised at altitudes above 10,000 feet, the *changla* sheep produces some of the longest woolen fibers of any sheep in the world. Though coarse, this wool is incredibly strong—ideal for Tibetan carpets.

As full of yawns as sleepy summertime can be, it is not a time to forget the ever-wakeful gods. On the full moon in August, Hindu dhamis gather to shake and tremble, to exchange energy in a powerful ritual devoted to the spirits.

At an ancient Bonpo holy place—a "power spot"—dhamis, clad only in loin cloths and holding bronze bells, wade into the swift, icy current of the Karnali River. Splashing water over their slender naked bodies, they emerge, dripping with sacred powers, before wrapping their heads in fresh white turbans.

Solemnly, the *chillum*—a native pipe—is passed, each dhami sharing the bonds of brotherhood in a communal smoke. Falling into a trance, the dhamis unwind their turbans with a jerk of their rolling heads, shaking out their long oiled locks and even longer braids. The braids, blessed with the body's most sacred power, are wrapped so tightly with silver thread that they tremble like a frenzied mass of snakes.

Twirling in trancelike dervishes, the dhamis press foreheads together and touch faces with trembling hands. Chhetri women gather to hold hands in sisterhood. Giggling, shuffling in the dirt as they sing, they celebrate the last days of summer before picking up the pestles for the pounding work of fall.

Crisp breezes course through the night, and the slow buzz of dancing bumblebees grows fainter as the fields ripple golden. A leaf drops to the ground and is blown away. On a distant cliff, a woman bends, digging potatoes. Seeking a friend of wisdom, Tom and I travel to Pema Lama's remote hermitage for our last goodbyes of the season.

Over a year has passed since I joined Tom in Humla, and with the fading of summer it is time to leave. Pema, a lama who has spent seven years in solitude, chants to a host of buddhas to protect us on our long journey home. His prayers echo in whispers before merging with the roar of the Karnali River below. A reverberation from his chants lingers, hovering over the canyon, hesitant and haunting.

Will Humla's rhythm of existence vanish, or will it remain hidden, as it has for centuries? Where is the lama we burned one winter's day? Where do the seasons go when their time has passed?

For a moment, Pema gazes reflectively out his window before churning butter into our tea. His eyes are wistful with the realization that his way of life, the way of the people of Humla, is destined to perish. This small cultural eddy will eventually be transformed by contact with modern technology and modern ways.

Or will it? Can Humla retain its soul while adopting Western technology? Maybe the modern world can learn from Humla as Humla will learn from the modern world.

Arriving at an ancient Bonpo ritual site beside the Karnali River, Hindu *dhamis* undress for the Janai Purnima ritual purification bath. Scooping up water with bronze bells, the dhamis cleanse themselves. The bath acts to renew the dhamis' vows and commitment to their sacred duties while evoking their initial purification bath in Lake Manaswarvor.

The villagers of Simikot parade to the local temple. The procession commences the Janai Purnima festival—an important preharvest ceremony in which *dhamis* reinforce bonds of brotherhood among themselves while rejuvenating bonds with the gods to insure a good harvest.

The oldest *pujari* in Simikot. Steeped in the wisdom of Humla's folk Hindu tradition, the pujari acts as translator of the gods who possess the *dhamis* during trance.

Inside the temple of the local deity Barpole, the congregation of *dhamis* peacefully share a ritual smoke of the *chillum,* waiting for the gods to descend and possess them.

Once the gods have received offerings and given blessings insuring a good harvest, the solemn mood changes to joyful celebration. Janai Purnima is the last chance to have fun before the hard work of harvest begins. To the beat of the drums, married Chhetri women, sing and dance, arm in arm.

Pema Lama, a Buddhist hermit who has spent the last seven years in solitude, pauses from churning salt-butter tea in his remote cliff-ledge hermitage. From his guru he has learned esoteric Tantric methods of training his mind to find peace—the wisdom of emptiness. To overcome his fear of death, Pema Lama meditates under waterfalls, on the edges of cliffs, and beside grave sites. Not until Pema has achieved an enlightened state will he leave the hermitage to give his compassion and wisdom to others.

Late monsoon clouds mask Humla's high Himalayas and ancient way of life.

Tibetan greeting and farewell: exchanging energies with the touch of the head, master, with open hands, receives his disciple, who holds his hands in a gesture of offering.

194

Despite the fragile nature of their mountain existence,
the Bhotias, Thakuris, and Chhetris celebrate.
Life is hard and short. Each moment is precious.
We bowed and touched heads.
Like a flash of lightning in a summer cloud
our time in Humla vanished.

GLOSSARY

The spelling of these Tibetan, Nepalese, and Sanskrit words has been phoneticized for ease in pronunciation. Tibetan words in particular have many different spellings. N: Nepalese word; T: Tibetan word; S: Sanskrit word.

Agni (N) Ancient Hindu god of fire.

Alchi (T) Protector goddess of Limi.

bahini (N) Little sister.

bardo (T) A forty-nine day intermediate state between life and death.

Barpole (N) Ancient local Hindu deity of Simikot and Brassi; said to have come from the South.

Bhavani (N) Folk Hindu goddess.

Bhotia (N) High-mountain people of Mongolian stock; Tibetan-speaking people living in the northern Himalayas.

bodhisattva (S) A person who has experienced enlightenment but who has taken a special vow to continue to be reborn in order to deliver others from suffering by aiding them to attain enlightenment.

Bon (T) Ancient pre-Buddhist religion of Tibet characterized by the practice of sorcery and animism. Bon eventually incorporated Iranian and Savite gnostic teachings, archaic shamanism, and Manichaeism into its beliefs.

Bonpo (T) Practitioner of the Bon religion.

chang or **chhang** (T) Mountain beer of fermented grain, usually barley or millet.

changla (T) High-altitude sheep known for its long-fiber wool.

Chhetri (N) The Hindu warrior caste, second only in status to Brahmans.

chillum (N) A small upright native Nepali pipe made from wood or stone.

chirpi (T) Dried cheese used in winter stews and as trail food.

Chitaloe (N) Ancient Hindu Humla festival commemorating the rite of spring. Fertile women sing and dance around the pole of the village deity, asking for good luck with the spring planting.

chobundi (N) Native Nepalese shirt worn by women and designed to accommodate breast-feeding.

chorten (T) Small Buddhist shrine containing religious relics.

chuba (T) Thick Tibetan coat.

damais (N) Caste of tailors who form makeshift bands to play religious music for weddings and other occasions.

damaru (N) A hand-held drum with leather thongs attached used in tantric ritual; formerly made from human skulls with human skin as a reminder of the body's impermanence.

daura surwal (N) Native Nepali dress for men consisting of a tie-wrap shirt extending to the thighs, and pants tight at the calf, baggy at the waist.

dhami (N) A soothsayer and sorcerer; a man who becomes possessed by lineage gods.

dhara (N) Bathing site; spring.

Dharma (T) The teaching of the Buddha; moral law, truth, and religion.

dharmapala (S), **chokyong** (T) Protectors of the faith.

dharamsala (N) Public resthouse for pilgrims.

dodchag (T) A vice causing worldly attachment.

doko or **docco** (N) A basket often carried on the head, secured by means of a strap.

dorge (T) A ritual scepter or thunderbolt, symbol of the absolute, the male, skill.

drilbu or **tilbu** (T) A bell symbolizing wisdom and emptiness; used in Tibetan Tantric ritual for exorcisms. The drilbu is the female counterpart to the dorge, and the sound symbolizes impermanence.

drokpa (T) Tibetan nomad; "dweller of the black tent."

dzo (T), **dhopa** (N) Sterile male offspring of a nak (female yak) and bull used as a pack and plow animal.

dzomo (T) Female offspring of a male yak and cow.

dzopkio (T), **jhuma** (N) Female offspring of a nak (female yak) and bull, prized for its high yield of milk and its docile temperament.

Eppi (T) Nickname meaning "Grandma."

gao or **gau** (T) Charm box or portable shrine; often elaborately decorated in silver and gold, it contains religious relics.

godzchoom (T) Turquoise- , coral- , and pearl-studded headdress; the tail of the godzchoom is normally hidden beneath a cape, so that the wealth of the wearer is unknown. Common headdress for Buddhist brides of western Himalayas.

gokpur (T) Wooden bowl made from the knot of a tree.

gompa or **gonpa** (T) Monastery; "house of meditation."

Gura (T) Local deity of the Bhotia village of Brassi.

Ilsa (T) Bon deity of the Bhotia village of Bargaon.

Janai Purnima (N) August full-moon celebration. In Humla, dhamis fall into a trance and renew ties of brotherhood among themselves and with the gods to insure a prosperous fall harvest.

jethi (N) Oldest sister.

Kabah (N) Arbiter and translator at trading fairs.

Kalo Silto (N) Local Hindu folk deity of upper Simikot village.

Kalyal (N) Thakuri dynasty that ruled in Humla after the fall of the Malla dynasty in the fourteenth century; ruled until the Gurkha conquest and unification of Nepal in 1768.

kami or **khamis** (N) Blacksmith caste of Nepal; associated with the fire god Agni.

kanchi (N) Fourth or youngest sister.

kangling (T) Thigh-bone horn used in Tantric ritual; sounds of the instrument drive away evil spirits.

kata, khata, or **cotta** (T) Tibetan Buddhist ceremonial blessing scarf.

kera (T) Belt or sash.

Khas, Kasia, or **Khasiyas** (S) An Indo-Aryan tribe who, in Vedic times, had not adopted Brahmanical ritual; principal inhabitants of regions west of Kashmir and in Nepal.

khola (N) River or stream.

kukuri (N) Traditional Nepali knife; long and curved, it is best known as the weapon of the Gurkha soldiers.

lama (T) Master, spiritual preceptor; Tibetan Buddhist monk. In Sanskrit, a guru.

latto (N) Cretin.

lekh (N) Mountain pass.

lhakpa (T) Sheepskin jacket.

Lobsong (T) "The blessed one"—a common Tibetan name.

lungta (T) "Windhorse"; Tibetan Buddhist prayer flag believed to transport the word of the dharma.

lutok (T) Pitch-pine kindling used as a source of light.

Mahakala (T) Chief dharmapala, protector deity; wrathful form of Avalokiteshvara, "protector of the tent"; Tibetan form of the Hindu god Shiva.

mah-jongg (Chinese) A game of Chinese origin played with 136 or 144 pieces marked in suits. The object of the game is to build combinations or sets by drawing, discarding, and exchanging pieces.

maili (N) Second-eldest sister.

Manaswarvor (N) Sacred lake in Tibet beside Mt. Kailash; origin of the Brahmaputra.

mandala (S), **chilkor** (T) Magic or sacred circle used in Tantric meditation and ritual; symbol of collective consciousness.

Mani (T) Masked spring festival ceremony.

manichorkor (T) Prayer wheel containing mantras; each revolution is believed to spin the prayers skyward to heaven.

mantra (S) "Instrument of the mind"; short verse or collection of syllables used to evoke a deity or gain protection against evil forces, or used as an object of meditation; prayer formula, chant, or spell.

Masta (N) Animistic, pre-Hindu religion of the native Khas people.

mela (N) Festival, celebration, or gathering in the middle hills of Nepal.

naga (S), **klu** (T) Serpent deity.

nangpa (T) "Interior person"; Buddhist.

Nyingmapa (T) The oldest of the Tibetan sects, the Nyingmapas are the "red hats" who claim Padmasambhava as their founder. Still greatly influenced by Tantric and Bon practices, the Nyingmapa lineage is characterized by its magical and mystical practices.

Nyinba (T) "People of the sunny valley"; Bhotia ethnic group of Humla living in Brassi, Latok, Torpu, Bargaon, and Limithang.

palpur (N) Sour yellow buckwheat.

pho-la (T) Lineage clan god.

phurba (T) Sacred dagger.

phyugs lhas spon bdun (T) "Gods of the flocks."

puja (N) Ritual offerings to the gods.

pujari (N) Wise man chosen by the dhami to act as translator during the dhami's possession; the pujari offers puja items and makes the animal sacrifice under the direction of the dhami.

puri (T) Bhotia fried-dough delicacy.

puro (T) Wooden teacup made from the knot of a tree.

ronglu (T) Pack sheep of Humla; ronglu produce lower-quality wool than the changla sheep, but can survive in low altitudes.

sangha (S) "Assemblage"; the order or community of Buddhist monks, nuns, and laity.

Sakyapa (T) "People of the gray earth"; Tibetan Buddhist sect founded by Marpa in the eleventh century.

shaili (N.) Third-eldest sister.

sho mo (T.) Prophecy or divination made by casting dice or mani beads and consulting texts.

tarchok (T) Prayer-flagpole; also the distinctive topknot hairdo worn by Bhotia men of Humla.

topi (N) Native cap worn by Nepalese men.

torma (T) Ritual food offering; sculpture made of roasted barley flour decorated with butter designs.

tozoms (T) Wooden butter churners.

tsampa (T) Ground roasted barley flour.

tsoompas (T) Native Bhotia footwear elaborately embroidered.

Vajrayana (S) Tantric Buddhism.

zee (T) Mud stone with patterns (it is believed) made by lightning bugs thousands of years ago; worn by Tibetans to protect against disaster during thunder and lightning storms.